THE GREEN BELTS

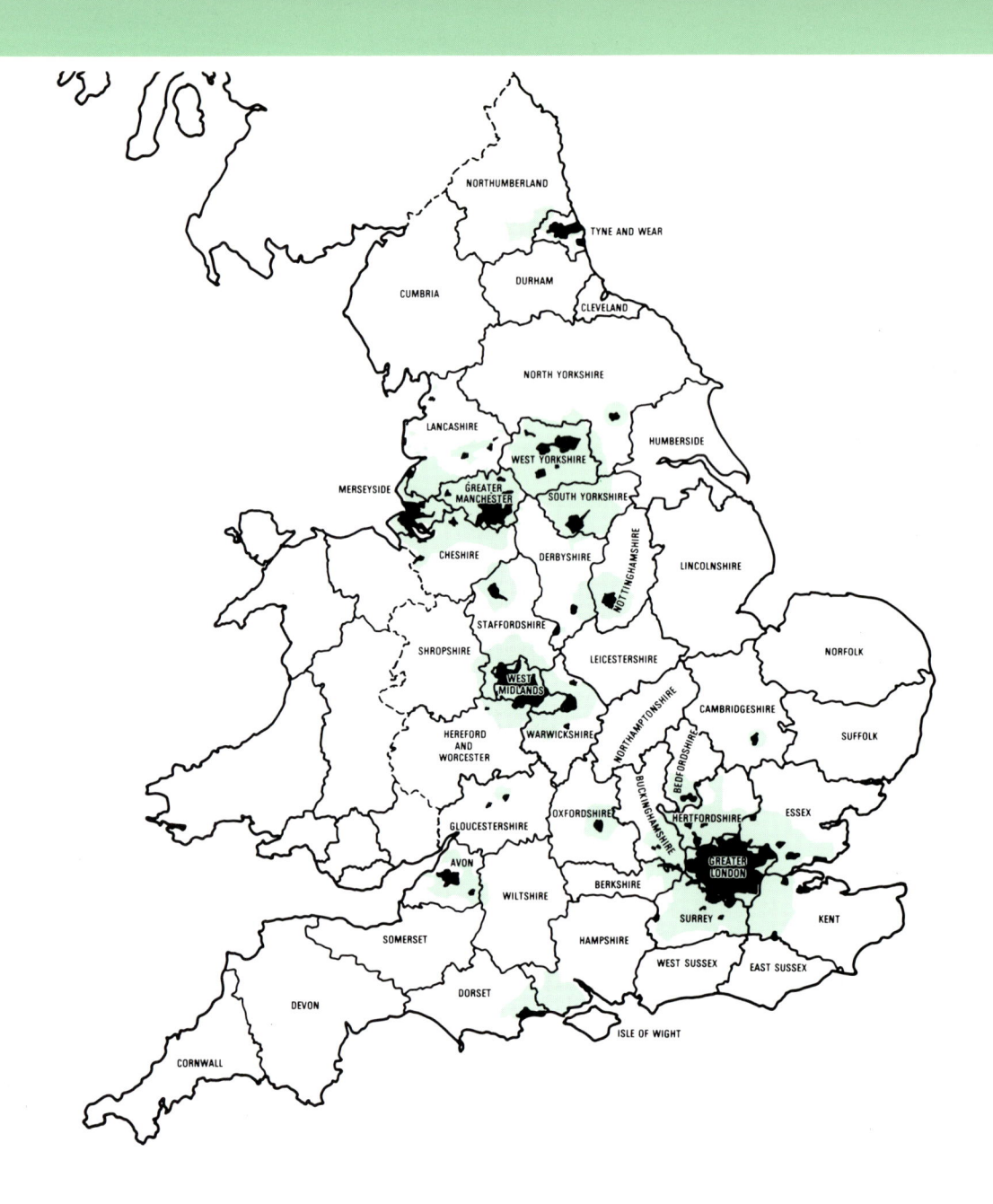

Approved Green Belts

	Acres (approx)
Tyne & Wear	200,000
Lancaster & Fylde Coast	5,750
York	50,000
South & West Yorkshire	800,000
Greater Manchester, Central Lancs, Merseyside, Wirral	750,000
Stoke-on-Trent	125,000
Nottingham, Derby	200,000
Burton – Swadlincote	2,000
West Midlands	650,000
Cambridge	26,550
Gloucester, Cheltenham	20,000
Oxford	100,000
London	1,200,000
Avon	150,000
SW Hampshire/SE Dorset	220,000
Total	**4,495,300**

Frontispiece: Approved Green Belts – based on Structure Plan key diagrams, September 1987

DEPARTMENT OF THE ENVIRONMENT

THE GREEN BELTS

LONDON: HER MAJESTY'S STATIONERY OFFICE

Acknowledgements

Maps The frontispiece map of approved Green Belts is taken from Planning Policy Guidance Note 2 (HMSO, 1988).

Figure 1 is derived from the Second Report of the Greater London Regional Planning Committee 1933 and the Greater London Plan 1944.

Figures 15 and 16 and the map of London's Green Belt at the back of the booklet have been produced for this booklet by the Cartographic Services Division of the Department of the Environment.

Photographs Many of the photographs in this booklet of sites in the Green Belt have been taken from the same view points used for photographs in the original 1962 edition; some new photographs have been added.

Figures 2 and 4 are reproduced by courtesy of St Albans Sand and Gravel, and Figure 5 by courtesy of Mr G Dyer.

Figure 17 – Simon Crouch
Figure 22 – Skyscan
Figure 23 – Martin Page Photography

All other photographs, including the photograph on the front cover, were taken specially for this booklet by Mr Charlie Waite of Landscape Only.

Apart from Figures 2 and 4, all maps and photographs in this booklet are Crown Copyright.

Front cover photo: Box Hill, Surrey.
Map inside back cover: London's Green Belt.

© Crown Copyright 1988
First Published 1988

ISBN 0 11 752143 4

Contents

		Page
Foreword by the Secretary of State for the Environment		6
1	Introduction	8
	What is a Green Belt?	
	The need for Green Belts.	
	Where is a Green Belt required?	
2	The Origins of Green Belts	9
	The Greater London Regional Planning Committee.	
	The Green Belt Act of 1938.	
	The Greater London Plan, 1944.	
	The Town and Country Planning Act, 1947.	
	Green Belts in the provinces.	
	Green Belts today.	
3	Restrictions on Building in a Green Belt	13
4	The Use of Land in a Green Belt	14
5	Defining and Safeguarding a Green Belt	16
	Structure Plans.	
	Local Plans.	
	Keeping a Green Belt open.	
6	London's Green Belt	17
	Its establishment.	
	Its topography.	
7	Provincial Green Belts	26
8	The Implications of a Green Belt	32
	The pressure on Green Belts.	
	The allocation of building land.	
	Review of development plans.	
	The journey to work.	
	Urban regeneration.	
9	The Maintenance and Improvement of a Green Belt	35
	The appearance of a Green Belt.	
	The role of the individual.	
Annex	Control over Development in Green Belts	38

Foreword by the Secretary of State for the Environment The Rt Hon Nicholas Ridley MP

This booklet was first published in 1962. I have decided to publish a new edition of it, not because our Green Belt policy has changed but because it demonstrates the continuity of that policy and our strong commitment to the Green Belts. I hope it will also remind people that Green Belts are something special. They serve specific purposes and they need to be carefully defined and firmly maintained.

The Green Belt idea had its origin long before the last war but it was not until the Green Belt (London and Home Counties) Act of 1938 that it was embodied in legislation. 1988 marks the 50th anniversary of that Act.

In preparing this new edition we found that very little in the text of the original version needed to be revised. After 25 years we have had to bring the factual and historical parts up to date, and the most important feature is that since 1979 we have more than doubled the total area of approved Green Belts. They now cover some 4,500,000 acres, and the London Green Belt has been increased to 1,200,000 acres. This booklet, like its predecessor, is mainly concerned with the London Green Belt but it also deals briefly with the Green Belts that have now been established in other parts of the country.

The basic Green Belt policy and its original purposes have not changed. But in the 1962 booklet there was a lot of emphasis on 'decentralisation' out of London and the other conurbations to New Towns, some of them within the Green Belts. We now put much more emphasis on the *regeneration* of the older urban areas and on the *re-use* of urban land. The purposes of the Green Belts were defined in 1954 as 'to check the further growth of a large built-up area; to prevent neighbouring towns from merging into one another; or to preserve the special character of a town'. In 1984 we added a fourth policy objective – 'assisting in urban regeneration'. Our Green Belt policy is now matched with our policies for the renewal and improvement of the inner cities.

Our Green Belt policy also has to be linked with positive policies providing for houses and jobs in areas outside the Green Belts. All development needs cannot be met within the existing built-up areas, and the Green Belt concept would be far less effective if it were applied everywhere that is not already developed. Outside the Green Belts we have policies for preserving the open countryside, National Parks, Areas of Outstanding Natural Beauty and other statutorily protected areas. But good planning has to provide for development too, and in ways that do least harm to the local environment.

The broad extent of the approved Green Belts has now been established in the county structure plans. But those plans show the Green Belts in very broad brush terms. The detailed boundaries have to be defined in local plans, which the local planning authorities are responsible for preparing and which are subject to formal procedures for public consultation and adoption. So it is disappointing to find that more than 30 years after local authorities were first invited to define Green Belts in development plans, large areas are still without a local plan and the precise boundaries have been left undefined. This provides no guidance to builders as to where development will and will not be allowed, and no assurance to local people who are left in similar uncertainty. I am issuing new advice to local planning authorities saying that I want to see full coverage of local plans, particularly in those areas where there are strong pressures for development and especially where the Green Belt boundaries have still not been clearly defined.

I hope that this booklet will demonstrate the success of the Green Belt policy and the pleasure that these wide open spaces around our great cities afford to millions of people. We must ensure that the Green Belts remain firmly in place for future generations.

1 Introduction

This Section is reproduced from the 1962 booklet, with the addition of the fourth objective of Green Belt policy that was introduced in 1984 – 'assisting in urban regeneration'.

What is a Green Belt? A Green Belt is an area of land, near to and sometimes surrounding a town, which is kept open by permanent and severe restriction on building. The form it takes depends on the purposes it is intended to serve. If it is wanted to prevent two nearby towns from joining up, all that is necessary is a sufficiently wide belt of open country between them, leaving the towns free to expand in other directions. More often, the purpose is to limit the expansion of a town and a virtually continuous belt all round it will be needed. There are also some groups of towns which are tending to merge into one solid urban mass. In such a case the Green Belt is partly a series of buffers of open land between the towns and partly a belt around the whole group.

The need for Green Belts The idea of a belt of open land around towns goes back to ancient times. Much of this land was used for growing food for the townspeople or pasturing their cattle but some of it provided space for recreation, for fairs and fights, sports and games and public occasions. This open belt served as a barrier against the spread of disease and as an exposed area which an attacking enemy would have to cross to reach the city walls. Modern transport now brings food to the city from far afield and permits the citizen to roam widely for his recreation. Modern medicine and modern housing have taken the terror from infectious diseases and walls have long been useless as defences. Then why should not the city be allowed to grow unchecked?

The answer is that some towns are already far too big for the comfort or the pleasure of the citizens, while others tend to merge with one another and need to be prevented from doing so. Many towns have expanded rapidly during the last hundred years and particularly since the advent of motor traffic. Some have coalesced with others to form huge conurbations where building seems endless and the boundary between different communities has become no more than a line on a map. Main roads have been lined with houses on both sides, to the detriment of traffic, and the distinction between town and country has become blurred. All these are the consequences of sprawl, which it is the primary purpose of a Green Belt to prevent.

The secondary purpose is perhaps better understood and appreciated. It is to provide opportunity to escape from the noise, congestion and strain of city life and to seek recreation in the countryside. Sometimes people may want to take part in organized games or sports or to pursue some scientific or artistic study or interest. More often they are content just to ramble or ride with no other object than to enjoy the scenery, fresh air and sunshine.

Where is a Green Belt required? By no means all towns need a Green Belt. In the normal way, planning authorities have adequate powers to control the growth of towns while maintaining a sharp distinction between town and country.

Mr. Duncan Sandys, who was then the Minister of Housing and Local Government, listed three reasons for the establishment of a Green Belt when he addressed a circular to local authorities on 3rd August, 1955. These three reasons were: (*a*) to check the growth of a large built-up area; (*b*) to prevent neighbouring towns from merging into one another; or (*c*) to preserve the special character of a town.

His successor, Mr. Henry Brooke, emphasized the permanent nature of Green Belts and the limited circumstances where they are applicable when, on 5th July, 1960, he said: *'The right principles are that a Green Belt should be established only where there is a clear need to contain the growth of a town within limits which can be defined at the time; and the limits of the belt should be carefully drawn so as not to include land which it is unnecessary to keep permanently open for the purpose of the Green Belt'*.

In 1984 the Government added a fourth objective to Green Belt policy – 'assisting in urban regeneration'. The aim is that by firmly maintaining the Green Belts, and preventing outward expansion, developers and others will be encouraged to turn their attention to opportunities for renewal and redevelopment within the urban areas. There is ample evidence that this policy is working.

2 The Origins of Green Belts

This Section is reproduced from the 1962 booklet, with updating of the last paragraph and the addition of the final passage on Green Belts today.

The first known attempt in this country to establish a Green Belt was a royal proclamation of Queen Elizabeth I in 1580, forbidding any new building on a new site within three miles of the city gates of London. The purposes were stated to be to ensure an abundance of cheap food and to mitigate the effects of an outbreak of plague. A similar proclamation was made by James I and in 1657 the Commonwealth Parliament passed an Act to limit the amount of building within ten miles of London by requiring new houses to have at least 4 acres of land.

No more legislative action was taken until the present century, though several suggestions were made for limiting the growth of the metropolis and establishing a belt of open country to be used either for agriculture or recreation.

The Greater London Regional Planning Committee In the 1920s the need to limit the spread of London became once more the concern of government. Electric power had freed many industries from having to be on the coalfields and they were attracted to the huge consumer market of London which, at the same time, provided skilled and versatile workpeople and a good distribution centre. Unemployment in the industrial north and in South Wales sent many journeying to London to work in the new light industries springing up in and around the capital.

The population increased rapidly and the ever-expanding transport services enabled people to live further and further from their place of work. Something had to be done. So in 1927 Mr. Neville Chamberlain, who was then the Minister of Health, set up the Greater London Regional Planning Committee. In addressing the first meeting of the Committee he asked them, amongst other things, to consider whether London should *'be provided with something which might be called an agricultural belt, as has often been suggested, so that it would form a dividing line between Greater London as it is and the satellites or fresh developments that might take place at a greater distance'*.

At an early stage in the Committee's deliberations their technical adviser, Sir Raymond Unwin, impressed on them the urgent need to reserve land for the recreation of Londoners. There were far too few playing fields within reach of the built-up area, suitable land was rapidly being taken for building and the additional population increased the demand. Instead of an agricultural belt, he suggested a girdle of open space to provide a reserve for the deficiency of playing fields near to the centre. He urged that building beyond this girdle should be planned against a background of open space instead of planning open space against a background of unlimited building land, as current legislation compelled (Fig.1).

The Green Belt Act of 1938 The economic crisis of the late twenties and the early thirties stopped for the moment any effective action to realize London's Green Belt, but it barely checked the growth of Greater London. In the late thirties the rate of building rose to a peak and 'development' engulfed whole towns and villages. Some of the Home Counties had already acquired land to prevent the spread of building but it was the London County Council who, at the request of the Regional Planning Committee, took the initiative towards realizing Unwin's 'green girdle'. In 1935 they put forward a scheme (which owed much to Lord Morrison of Lambeth) 'to provide a reserve supply of public open spaces and of recreational areas and to establish a Green Belt or girdle of open space lands, not necessarily continuous, but as readily accessible from the completely urbanized area of London as practicable'. The Council offered grants to the Councils of the Home Counties and other local authorities towards the cost of acquiring or preserving land for inclusion in this green girdle.

Within a few months arrangements had been made to acquire or preserve about 18,000 acres but it was soon found that the existing powers of the authorities concerned had to be supplemented. A Bill was presented to allow land to be acquired by agreement or declared to be part of the Green Belt, and to provide that no such land should be sold or built upon without the consent of the responsible Minister and of the contributing authorities. In due course this Bill became the Green Belt (London and Home Counties) Act, 1938. Altogether, up to the present, about 35,500 acres have been kept open by means of the London County Council's scheme and the 1938 Act.

The Greater London Plan, 1944 In 1944 Professor Sir Patrick Abercrombie completed an advisory plan for Greater London which he had been invited to prepare by the first Minister of Town and Country Planning. Abercrombie discerned in the apparently amorphous sprawl of London faint indications of a

Fig. 1 Early proposals for a London Green Belt

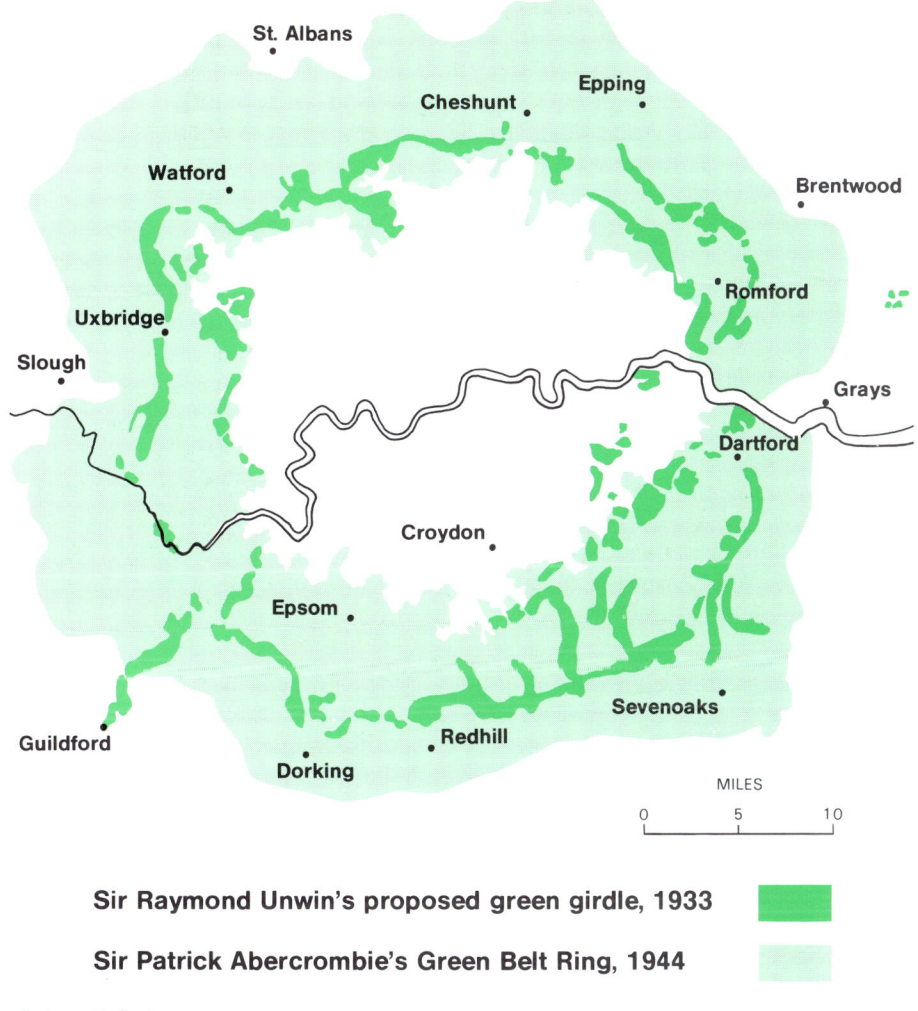

Sir Raymond Unwin's proposed green girdle, 1933

Sir Patrick Abercrombie's Green Belt Ring, 1944

Cartographic Services
Department of the Environment

structure of concentric rings and upon this he based his plan (Fig. 1). The main problem was the relief of congestion in the crowded 'inner ring' which he proposed should be chiefly met by the building of new towns and the expansion of existing towns in the fourth or 'outer country ring'. Between these lay the 'suburban ring' which was to remain virtually static and outside it the 'Green Belt ring'. This last he described as a 'zone with sufficient openness to have enabled attempts to be made to create a Green Belt, a zone in which the communities still maintain some semblance of distinct individuality'. Abercrombie proposed that, with certain exceptions for important manufacturing centres and immediate post-war housing, the expansion of existing communities should be strictly limited and no new centres established.

He saw it in much the same light as did the Scott Committee on Land Utilization in Rural Areas which reported in 1942, that is to say as a belt of open land girdling the built-up area in which in the main the normal rural and other activities appropriate to the district would continue undisturbed. Abercrombie proposed a belt of country about 5 miles deep with some wedges of open space penetrating the built-up area. Much of this land was privately owned and used for farming but most of that which had been bought under the 1938 Act and other publicly owned open spaces were included.

The specific proposals for this Green Belt were set out on the maps attached to Abercrombie's plan. They were considered in detail by all the authorities concerned and after amendment were embodied in the development plans of the local planning authorities. In the process the belt was widened to between 6 and 10 miles.

The Town and Country Planning Act, 1947 London was not the only city in the country to consider the provision of a Green Belt. Birmingham, Leeds and Sheffield had before the war acquired large areas of land for the purpose or had agreed with the owners that their land should be kept open. But these methods were expensive and it was not until the Town and Country Planning Act of 1947 came into force that the establishment of Green Belts around the major cities was really possible.

Under this Act any development of land required permission; so local planning authorities no longer needed to buy land to keep it open, they could simply refuse permission for it to be developed. Any resulting compensation was payable by the Government, so Green Belts could be established without fear of heavy compensation falling on local funds. Although the financial basis of the Act has since been amended these principles have been maintained. Millions of pounds have been spent by the Government on compensation and large areas around London and other great conurbations, which by now would otherwise have been swallowed up, have been kept as open country.

Green Belts in the provinces Until the middle 1950s the only formal proposal for an encircling Green Belt was that for London. On 26th April, 1955, the then Minister of Housing and Local Government, Mr. Duncan Sandys, said in the House of Commons: '*I am convinced that, for the well-being of our people and for the preservation of the countryside, we have a clear duty to do all we can to prevent the further unrestricted sprawl of the great cities*'.

He asked all local authorities concerned to consider the establishment of clearly defined Green Belts where that was desirable. Since then, the Green Belts have been established and incorporated in approved structure plans. These are briefly described on pages 26–32 and shown diagrammatically on the map at the front of this booklet.

Green Belts today Green Belts in approved structure plans now extend to nearly 4,500,000 acres in England. The London Green Belt is by far the largest and extends to about 1,200,000 acres. Since 1979 the total area of approved Green Belts has more than doubled.

The Government has made it abundantly clear that *The Government attaches great importance to the Green Belts, which have been an essential element of planning policy for more than three decades. The objectives of Green Belt policy and the related development control objectives set out in 1955 remain valid today* (Planning Policy Guidance Note No. 2, January 1988).

3 Restrictions on Building in a Green Belt

This Section is reproduced from the 1962 booklet, with the addition of the final paragraph.

The object of including land in a Green Belt is to keep it permanently open. Consequently there is a clear presumption against any new building and against any new employment which might create a demand for more building.

It is very difficult to get permission to build in a Green Belt. Anyone who wants to do so must be prepared to show either that the building is required for purposes appropriate to a Green Belt (e.g. for agriculture) or that there is some special reason why it should be allowed, despite the general presumption to the contrary. A cottage which simply fills a gap in an established village may well be permissible but it is not to be assumed that further houses will be allowed on land adjoining any that already exist. Nor is it enough to show that the building will be inconspicuous or will do no harm on the particular site, though these arguments can reinforce a case which has other merits. The Green Belt conception implies no further building except where there is a positive argument for allowing it.

Development which does not interfere with the open character of the land may be permissible. Buildings for sport or recreation, hospitals and similar institutions standing in extensive grounds, cemeteries and mineral working may be allowed. In such cases the decision is likely to turn on the need for the proposal as against any damage it will do to the rural appearance of the land.

As it is the intention that a Green Belt shall have a rural character, restrictions on building are somewhat similar to those applying to the ordinary countryside which lies beyond*. The main difference is that in the rural areas beyond the Green Belt it may be necessary at some time to allocate areas for building which may be quite extensive. Within the Green Belt the presumption is against any new building at any time, subject only to such limited exceptions as are stated in the development plan, or as may be specially approved in accordance with the preceding paragraphs.

This statement of Green Belt policy, as set out in the 1962 booklet, remains valid today. It was reinforced and supplemented in DoE Circulars 14/84 and 12/87, which have been incorporated in Planning Policy Guidance Note No. 2; an extract from that Note is reproduced in the Annex to this new edition of the 1962 booklet.

---

*Guidance on planning control in rural areas is given in the DoE booklet *Rural Enterprise and Development* (HMSO, 1987) and in Planning Policy Guidance Note No. 7 (HMSO, 1988).

4 The Use of Land in a Green Belt

This Section is reproduced from the 1962 booklet, with updating of the third paragraph.

The inclusion of land in a Green Belt does not give the public any rights of access which they would not otherwise enjoy. Most Green Belts include woods and forests, downs and commons, lakes and rivers, which attract people in large numbers and are maintained wholly or partly for public enjoyment. Though these are often extensive areas, they are a small part of the Green Belt as a whole, most of which remains privately owned and is predominantly farmland. Even though the townsman has no right of entry to such land, it is none the less precious to him for its natural beauty and quiet, which can be enjoyed from country lanes and public footpaths†.

Some Green Belts contain many fine country estates and mansions. Some of these are still private houses while others are used for schools, research institutions, staff colleges, field study centres and the like. Several of them are examples of great architecture and are popular places for a week-end visit. Planning authorities have powers to prevent the demolition of buildings of architectural or historic value but those powers do not help against dry rot and decay. The real problem of the preservation of these buildings is to find an economic use for them and that as often as not includes the use of the park, which may have been laid out in the first place by one of the great landscape architects of the 18th century.

There are, however, some activities which must take place in the Green Belt and are unsightly, at least for the time being. The working of minerals is an example. Chalk, gravel and clay are needed to make the cement, concrete and bricks of new roads and buildings and they can only be quarried where they occur in nature. The actual operation is temporary, though it may be noisy and intrusive, but the main problem arises after the minerals have been extracted. Worked-out gravel pits in the river valleys become flooded and may acquire a scientific value from the rare plants that grow there and the birds that make them their home. Others have been purposefully restored as nature reserves (Fig. 2), and some have been adapted for sailing, fishing and water sports of all kinds, for which there is an increasing demand (Fig. 3). Dry pits have sometimes been levelled and cultivated or they have been used for waste disposal and then restored for farming (Fig. 4) or used for playing fields.

There are also semi-urban uses of land, such as those concerned with public health, which are necessary to a city and have to be provided in the immediately surrounding countryside. Although their presence in the Green Belt is not ideal from the point of view of its recreational value they need not be unsightly. Reservoirs, indeed, can be an asset to the landscape and even a sewage disposal works can be assimilated by skilful planting and land formation.

---

†County Councils were required by the National Parks and Access to the Countryside Act, 1949, (and now by the Highways Act, 1980) to carry out a survey of public rights-of-way. Ordnance Survey Maps on a scale of 1/25,000 show these rights-of-way wherever the information is available.

Fig. 2 Nature reserve on restored sand and gravel workings in the Green Belt at Amwell near Ware, Hertfordshire

Fig. 3 Windsurfing in a flooded gravel pit at Wraysbury, Berkshire

Fig. 4 Sheep grazing on a restored landfill site at Hatfield quarry, Hertfordshire

5 Defining and Safeguarding a Green Belt

This Section, about incorporating Green Belts into development plans, has been brought up to date in the light of changes in the statutory provisions on development plans.

Structure Plans At the time when the original edition of this booklet was published in 1962, very few Green Belts, except for the London Green Belt, had been formally incorporated into the statutory development plans. The booklet gave advice on the preparation of initial 'sketch plans', which had to be submitted to the Minister of Housing and Local Government for approval, and the subsequent stages of incorporating them into development plans. Now all the Green Belts have been included in approved County structure plans. But structure plans show the Green Belts only in 'broad brush' terms. The detailed boundaries of Green Belts are defined in local plans prepared by the District planning authorities, or in some cases in Green Belt subject plans prepared by the Counties. In some areas, however, detailed Green Belt boundaries have not yet been defined in formally adopted local plans or subject plans. In some cases it is possible to trace the Green Belt boundary in old-style development plans prepared prior to the introduction of structure and local plans, but these are often out of date.

Local Plans The Secretary of State is urging on local planning authorities the importance of well prepared and up-to-date local plans as the basis for development control, particularly in areas that are under persistent pressure for new development, and especially in relation to the Green Belts where detailed boundaries have not yet been defined.

Now that the Green Belts have been established in approved structure plans, it is essential that the detailed boundaries should be clearly defined in local plans, so that it is clear which areas are covered by the special policies that apply to Green Belts and which are not. The long term protection that distinguishes the Green Belts must be maintained firmly and consistently, and both the Green Belt concept and that protection would be weakened unless they are firmly built into the statutory development plan.

Further advice on the definition of Green Belt boundaries is given in Planning Policy Guidance Note No. 2. In particular it gives the following advice:

> Once the general extent of a Green Belt has been approved it should be altered only in exceptional circumstances. If such an alteration is proposed the Secretary of State will wish to be satisfied that the authority has considered opportunities for development within the urban areas contained by and beyond the Green Belt. Similarly, detailed Green Belt boundaries defined in adopted local plans or earlier approved development plans should be altered only exceptionally. Detailed boundaries should not be amended or development allowed merely because the land has become derelict. On the outer edge of a Green Belt, readily recognisable features, such as roads, streams or belts of trees, should be used to define the boundaries.

Where detailed Green Belt boundaries have not yet been defined, local planning authorities are urged to complete this task. It is necessary to establish boundaries that will endure and they should be carefully drawn so as not to include land which it is unnecessary to keep permanently open. Otherwise there is a risk that encroachment on the Green Belt will have to be allowed in order to accommodate future development.

Keeping a Green Belt open When a Green Belt has been incorporated in the development plan of a local planning authority, it is their duty to carry out the policy prescribed in the plan. Development plans are firm in general principle but flexible in detail. They are reviewed and amended as and when necessary, usually every five to ten years. Planning authorities are bound to have regard to their development plans when they make a decision on an application for permission to build. If in so doing they intend to depart from the plan to a substantial extent, they must first notify the Secretary of State, who has the power to intervene if he thinks fit. These are necessary measures to preserve flexibility in detail and to provide for public debate on any substantial amendment to a development plan. They do not imply any wavering on the principle of maintaining a Green Belt as open country, a principle which has been firmly upheld by local planning authorities and successive Secretaries of State.

6 London's Green Belt

This Section has been rewritten to take account of the large extensions made to London's approved Green Belt since 1962.

Its establishment London's Green Belt was the first to be established, and is the largest, so it merits a full description. The creation of a Green Belt around the metropolis had been urged for many years, and had been given form in the Greater London Plan of 1944. That plan and its successors proposed not only the Green Belt but also the building of new towns and the expansion of existing towns in the surrounding counties, so as to ease the pressure for the outward expansion of London. It is these things, together with the firm planning policies which back the Green Belt designation in development plans, which have made London's Green Belt a reality. No physical changes nor public acquisition of the land are necessarily implied.

The approval in 1959 of the last of the development plans of the Home Counties made it possible to speak of London's Green Belt as an established fact and no longer as an elusive ideal. Since then, as the pressures of urban expansion and the threat of the coalescence of towns and villages have spread beyond the original Green Belt, so the area of the Green Belt has been extended. Today the approved Green Belt covers about 1,200,000 acres of the country around Greater London, an area more than twice as big as that approved in 1959. The extent of the

Metropolitan Green Belt, as established in 1959 and as now approved, is shown on the map at the end of the booklet.

Its topography London's Green Belt is by no means a topographic entity and derives its unity solely from the metropolis which it surrounds. It can, however, be considered in seven sectors, each of which has some coherence and its own character and scenery. They are linked together by the London orbital motorway (M25), itself a feature in the landscape, which affords motorway users many fine views into the countryside of the Green Belt (Fig. 5). Together with other recent road improvements it has brought better access to the Green Belt's varied recreational resources.

The south eastern sector contains the Darenth Valley from Sevenoaks to Dartford (Fig. 6) and extends eastward to the valley of the River Medway, and southward into the Weald as far as Tunbridge Wells. The Thames-side area is fragmented by mineral workings, vacant or damaged land, but the remainder is mainly chalk country with some charming villages and magnificent beech woods. Lullingstone Park near Eynsford, Knole House south east of Sevenoaks and Chevening House and park to the north west of the town are popular with visitors to the area.

The southern sector is based on the scarp of the North Downs (Fig. 7) which stretches from Sevenoaks to Guildford with the ancient trackway known as the Pilgrims' Way clinging to its face. Both the Downs and the greensand hills to the south afford magnificent views over the Weald, while the occasional white scar in the chalk gives a dramatic quality to the view of the Downs themselves when seen

Fig. 5 The M25 in the Green Belt near Badgers Mount between Swanley and Sevenoaks, Kent

Fig. 6 The Darenth Valley, Kent

Fig. 7 The Buckland Hills near Reigate, Surrey, part of the scarp of the North Downs

Fig. 8 Leith Hill, the centre of a favourite recreational area in Surrey owned by the National Trust

from below. The scarp in Surrey and the Leith Hill area (Fig. 8) to the south west of Dorking is part of an Area of Outstanding Natural Beauty. North of the scarp there is a substantial area of open country, mostly in Kent, which is well-wooded and even now in part relatively remote. To the west of this there was more extensive development at the time when the Green Belt was set up and the green areas are fragmented, though in some parts there are fine views to the north over London, notably from Banstead and Epsom Downs. The gap cut in the chalk by the River Mole north of Dorking is particularly attractive and of special interest to geographers (Fig. 9).

The south western sector, which extends from Leatherhead and Guildford southwards as far as the Hampshire border and northwards to the Thames and to Sunningdale, has no unifying topographical feature. It is relatively flat land drained by the rivers Wey and Mole which in their meanderings towards the Thames afford many opportunities for canoeing, fishing and other water sports. It contains a number of well-known and much frequented commons, such as Bookham, Wisley (Fig. 10), Ockham, Esher and Chobham, as well as Horsell Common, which H G Wells chose as the place where the Martians land in 'The War of the Worlds'. There are several country houses and parks associated with famous people either as occupants or architects and landscape architects, including Claremont, Esher, designed by 'Capability' Brown for Lord Clive and Painshill, one of the earliest of the great 18th-century landscape gardens. Valuable green wedges thrust inwards to the Thames west of Molesey and to the Kingston bypass at Hook. On the other hand the sector is almost severed by a succession of towns along the main railway line to Woking.

Fig. 9 The Dorking-Leatherhead road from Box Hill, Surrey

Fig. 10 Wisley Common, Surrey – a favourite picnic place adjoining the Portsmouth Road

The western sector, from Sunningdale to Gerrards Cross, is the most seriously fragmented of all. Much of it lies in the flood plain of the Thames where the Green Belt serves mainly to prevent the coalescence of neighbouring communities. Major sources of employment on the western side of London, including Heathrow Airport, have always generated strong pressure for new development in this sector which the Green Belt has kept in check. On the right bank of the Thames near Runnymede the land rises and the Commonwealth Air Forces Memorial at Cooper's Hill affords a fine panorama reaching from Windsor Castle to the centre of London (Fig. 11). To the west, the Green Belt extends over the fine expanse of Windsor Great Park and along the Thames valley to Maidenhead, Marlow and as far as Wargrave. North of Slough, on a series of gravel terraces lying in a bite out of the Chiltern chalk there is some well-wooded country, much of it open for public enjoyment including Burnham Beeches, Black Park and Langley Park. Here also is Stoke Poges.

The western and north western sectors are linked by the valley of the River Colne flowing from Watford through Uxbridge to join the Thames at Staines. Large parts of this area are taken up by gravel pits and reservoirs, and by damaged landscape. Several local authorities acting jointly have established the Colne Valley Regional Park to safeguard the area from further urbanisation, to improve its environment and enhance its recreational value. Beyond the Colne Valley the north western sector is for the most part Chiltern chalk downland intersected by the valleys of the Misbourne, Chess (Fig. 12) and Gade (Fig. 13). The Green Belt extends across the Chilterns Area of Outstanding Natural Beauty as far as the escarpment running from Stokenchurch north westwards to Tring. There are few good roads between

Fig. 11 Runnymede and West Middlesex from the Commonwealth Air Forces Memorial at Cooper's Hill

Fig. 12 Latimer, in the Chess Valley, Buckinghamshire

Fig. 13 The Grand Union Canal in the Gade Valley near Watford

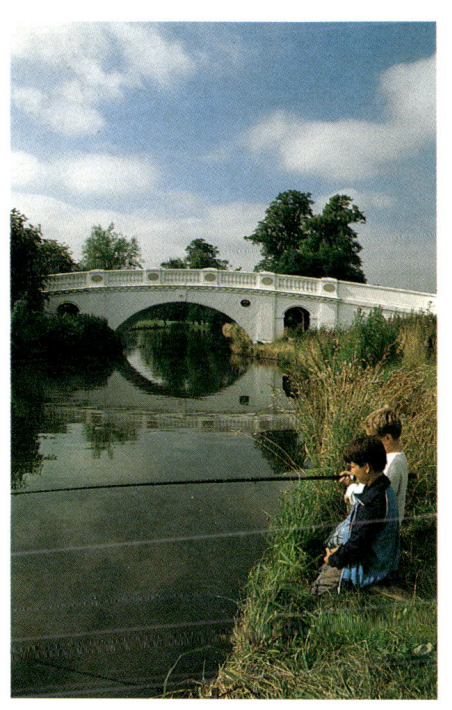

the valleys and the narrow tortuous lanes and occasional steep gradients help to maintain the rural character of the area. The existing built-up areas along the railway from Rickmansworth to Amersham interrupt the continuity of the Green Belt but not so badly as the almost continuous ribbon of building along the Gade Valley from Watford to Hemel Hempstead. This sector contains much of the land protected by purchase under the 1938 Act and earlier, as well as Moor Park in Hertfordshire.

The northern sector from Watford to Hoddesdon is for the most part gently rolling land on the London clay. Here also a large proportion of the original Green Belt was protected by acquisition. The inner boundary is prominently marked by the Elstree ridge and, north of Barnet, Dyrham Park and Wrotham Park maintain a sharp distinction between town and country. Further east, Hadley Common, Enfield Chase and Trent Park interpose a firm barrier against the outward spread of London. Near Hatfield the Green Belt comes up to the Lea Valley and includes Hatfield Park, with its historic mansion. Immediately to the east of the Park there is a pleasant rural area around Essendon and Bayford, which extends through Broxbourne Woods as far as the valley of the Lea where it flows southward to join the Thames. This sector of the Green Belt has been extended northwards to encircle, and separate, all the substantial towns of Hertfordshire, including the historic city of St Albans, the first Garden Cities of Letchworth and Welwyn and the post-war new towns of Hemel Hempstead, Hatfield and Stevenage.

Adjoining this sector is the Green Belt of south Bedfordshire, which includes within it the popular attractions of Dunstable Downs, Luton Hoo and Woburn

23

Fig. 14 In Monk Wood, Epping Forest

Fig. 15 Green Belts and Areas of Outstanding Natural Beauty in South East England outside London cover 42 per cent of the total land area

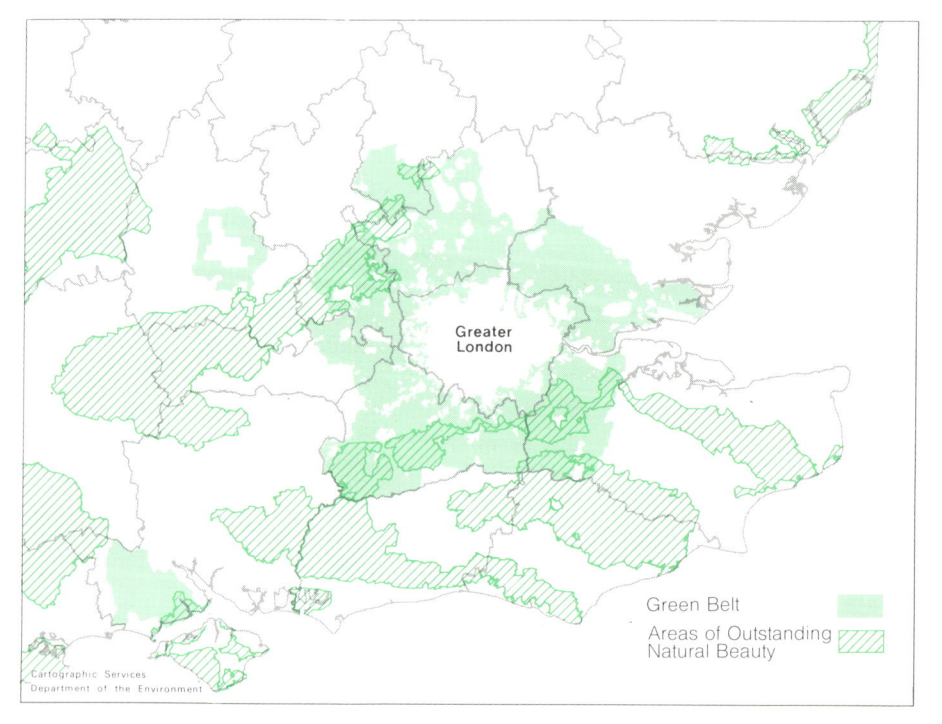

Park. The Green Belt serves to contain the urban areas of Luton, Dunstable and the other towns of southern Bedfordshire.

The north east sector comprises the remainder of the Green Belt from the Lea Valley to the Lower Thames. The Lea Valley is another area containing damaged landscape, where over the last 20 years much effort has been put into providing recreational amenities and conserving and enhancing the environment. The Lea Valley Regional Park Authority was established for this purpose. Perhaps the most prominent feature of this sector is Epping Forest, more than 5,000 acres of woodland vested in the City of London Corporation in 1878 after a long struggle against its enclosure (Fig. 14). Between the Forest on its ridge and the Lea Valley there is a fine wedge of open country from Harlow nearly to Chingford and including land once the manor of King Harold, who is said to have been buried at Waltham Abbey. To the east of Epping Forest there is a tongue of building stretching out along the Central Line as far as Epping but beyond lies the Roding Valley, a deep wedge of open country penetrating to Chigwell and through Hainault Forest to Barkingside. The Green Belt now extends over a wide tract of Essex farmland, from Hatfield Heath south eastwards across the Rodings, Chelmsford and eastwards between the River Crouch and Southend-on-Sea. In south Essex it is fragmented in places by the building that followed the railway lines to Brentwood, Basildon and Southend, but south of Brentwood the land is fairly open and a large part is low lying, drained to the Thames by the Mar Dyke. The Green Belt stops short of the Essex riverside industrial areas and former chalk quarries, where much regeneration and redevelopment is in progress.

Fig. 16 Urban areas in South East England outside London cover 12.6 per cent of the total land area

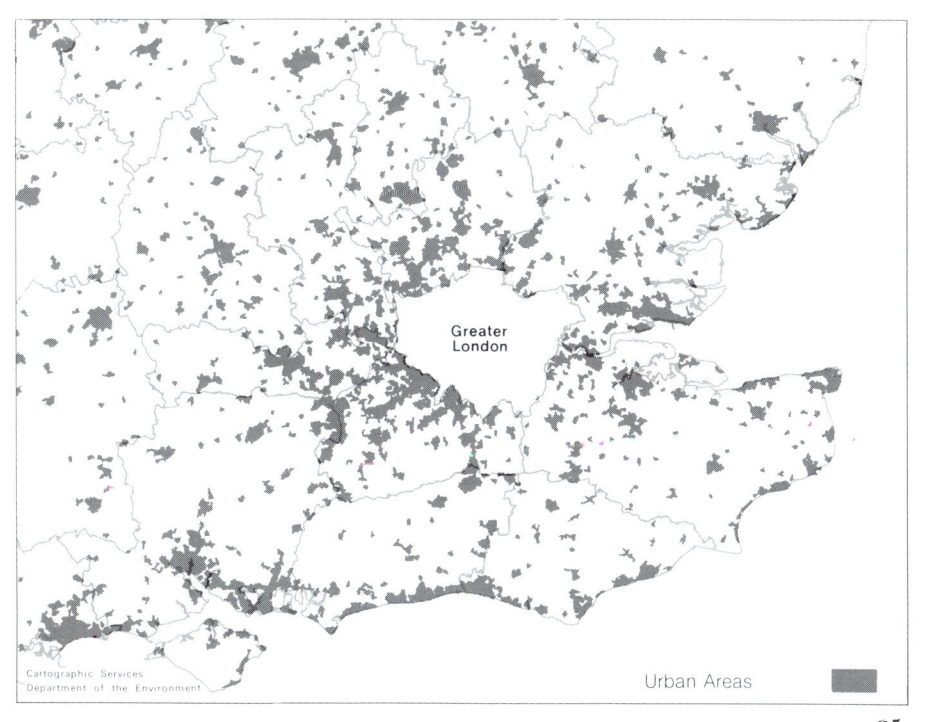

To sum up, London's Green Belt is an irregular and broken ring of open country around the great city, the use of which contributes in one form or another to the well-being of Londoners. It is as necessary today, but for different reasons, as in the days when London was dependent on the agriculture of the surrounding countryside. Increased leisure, higher standards of living, the greater strain of urban life and a growing desire for knowledge and understanding of the arts and sciences combine to invite Londoners to appreciate more and more the value of their Green Belt.

7 Provincial Green Belts

This Section has been revised to take account of the wide extensions to approved Green Belt since 1962.

When the 1962 booklet was published proposals for several of the provincial Green Belts were still in their formative stages. Since then, they have all been incorporated in approved structure plans and are shown diagrammatically on the map at the front of this booklet. These Green Belts now extend to a wide range of beautiful and diverse landscapes throughout England, while also serving the objectives of urban containment and regeneration.

Tyneside The boundaries of the Green Belt in Tyneside were extended in the Tyne and Wear Green Belt Local Plan, adopted in 1985. With the exception of a gap to its north east the Tyneside conurbation is surrounded by Green Belt. In merging with the substantial area of Green Belt in Northumberland, situated to the west and north of Newcastle (Fig. 17), a continuous Green Belt is formed embracing attractive countryside on both banks of the Tyne as far up as Hexham. To the south the Green Belt prevents the Tyneside conurbation from merging with that of Wearside.

York A Green Belt around York has been approved in principle for many years and a belt whose outer edge is about 6 miles from York City centre was formally approved in 1980 as part of the North Yorkshire County Structure Plan. Its main purpose is to safeguard the special character of the historic city, which might be endangered by unrestricted expansion. The bulk of the land in the Green Belt is good and pleasant farmland, providing links with open land running into the built-up area of the city.

West Yorkshire Conurbation This Green Belt was reviewed and approved in 1980 in the County Structure Plans for West and North Yorkshire. The Green Belt provides wedges of open land between the urban areas, a continuous band of generally open land within the core of the conurbation and a girdle to the conurbation as a whole. Its main purposes are to prevent uncontrolled growth of the urban areas and the coalescence of many separate settlements, to preserve the recreational and amenity value of areas of open land which extend from the countryside into the urban area and to preserve easy access to open country and outdoor recreation in pleasant surroundings. The Green Belt has contributed to the maintenance of the unusually open, and often attractive, character of this conurbation. Towards the outer edges of the belt much of the countryside is particularly scenic, especially in the hills and valleys to the west and north.

South Yorkshire Conurbation The broad extent of this Green Belt was reviewed and approved in 1979 in the South Yorkshire County Structure Plan. It is intended to prevent uncontrolled growth of the major urban areas of Sheffield, Rotherham, Doncaster and Barnsley, and the coalescence of the many smaller settlements which lie between them in a broad band of countryside stretching from the Peak District National Park in the west to Doncaster in the east. Sheffield was one of the first cities to consider the provision of a Green Belt in 1938 and, in 1983, it was the first District in the Yorkshire and Humberside Region to adopt a formal Green Belt subject plan. While the main purpose of this Green Belt is to prevent the merging of settlements, it has the advantage of protecting attractive countryside, particularly on the edge of the Pennines, while helping to preserve easy access to open country and outdoor recreation in pleasant surroundings.

Merseyside – Greater Manchester The Merseyside, Greater Manchester, Central Lancashire and North Cheshire Green Belts combine to form a belt around and between the two north west conurbations. Their purpose is to halt the outward spread and coalescence of the built-up areas and to preserve the identity and character of the many towns and settlements which make up the conurbations (Fig. 18). The Green Belts extend in a broad band, from the Ribble Valley in the

Fig. 17 Near Bywell, Northumberland – looking south over the valley of the River Tyne in the Tyneside Green Belt

Fig. 18 A picnic in the Green Belt at Pickmere, north Cheshire

Fig. 19 The Macclesfield Canal, Cheshire

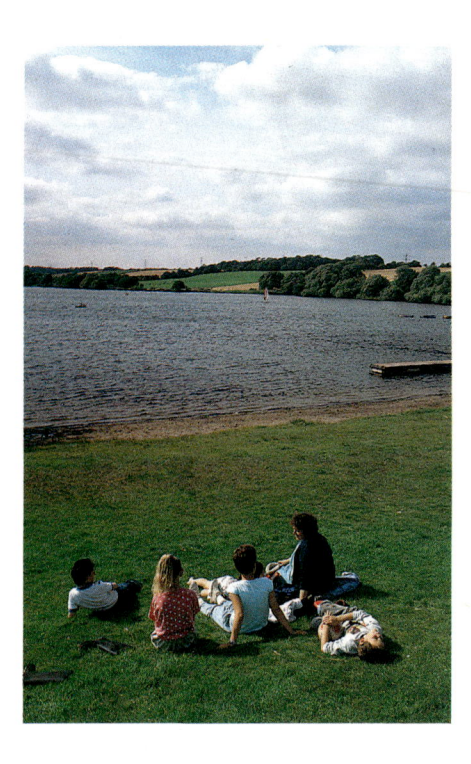

north to Chester in the south, and from the Lancashire coast in the west to the foothills of the Pennines in the east. An arm of the Central Lancashire Green Belt continues up the Calder Valley to encompass the towns of north east Lancashire. In each case the Green Belts help to reinforce policies for urban regeneration.

The character of the landscape varies greatly: from the flat, top quality farmland of south west Lancashire to the lush hills and valleys adjoining the Peak District National Park in north east Cheshire (Fig. 19). It includes the pleasant agricultural scenery of part of the Cheshire Plain, where there are several large areas of parkland and golf courses, and further west takes in magnificent views of the Dee Estuary and the Welsh Hills beyond. In north east Lancashire, the Green Belt includes land on the edge of industrial towns framed by views of Pendle Hill (part of the Forest of Bowland Area of Outstanding Natural Beauty) and of the South Pennine moors.

Much of the Green Belt within the conurbations is fragmented and contains derelict areas and the varied mixture of uses often found on the fringes of large towns. A feature of the Greater Manchester Green Belt is the inclusion of narrow fingers along several river valleys which bring countryside into the heart of built-up areas of the conurbation. Although some parts of these valleys have been used for industrial and other development in the past, large areas remain relatively unspoiled and the local authorities are working together to restore them and to exploit their potential for walking, riding and other informal recreational pursuits.

Lancashire Coast Small remaining areas of open land have been designated as Green Belt along the north Lancashire coast to prevent the merging of Blackpool,

Cleveleys, Lytham St Annes and other coastal towns, and to arrest the northward spread of Morecambe and Lancaster.

West Midlands The Green Belt has restrained the outward growth of the main built-up areas of Birmingham, Coventry and the Black Country; safeguarded surrounding countryside, some parts of which eg. the Lickey Hills and Cannock Chase are of high landscape value and popular places of outdoor recreation; maintained the separate character of individual towns like Stafford, Tamworth, Nuneaton, Redditch and Bromsgrove; preserved the special character of cities and towns like Lichfield, Warwick, Bridgnorth and Stratford upon Avon; and assisted in the regeneration of the older urban areas inside the conurbation. Green Belt protection has also been given to two strategic areas of open land inside the conurbation, one, the Sandwell Valley in the Black Country, the other Sutton Park in Birmingham because of the vital contribution these open areas make to the quality of the urban environment.

Derbyshire and Nottinghamshire The four Green Belts in Derbyshire were reviewed and approved in 1980 in the County Structure Plan. The South Derbyshire Green Belt prevents the coalescence of Burton on Trent and Swadlincote. Similarly the South East Derbyshire Green Belt prevents the coalescence of Derby and Nottingham and preserves the identity of Duffield, Belper, the Erewash Valley Towns and villages to the south and east of Derby. In the north of the County, the Green Belt for North East Derbyshire protects the open countryside between Sheffield and the settlements in the north east of the County, including Chesterfield (Fig. 20), while the North West Derbyshire Green Belt helps to maintain the separate identity of the north west Derbyshire towns and protects the

Fig. 20 Looking east towards Chesterfield over the Green Belt in north east Derbyshire from the Peak District National Park

very attractive open country north of Whaley Bridge between the borders of the Peak District National Park and Greater Manchester.

The County Structure Plan approved in 1980 set out the broad extent of the Nottinghamshire Green Belt. Much of the Green Belt is pleasant countryside and average to good farmland. Its main purpose is to prevent the uncontrolled growth of Nottingham in the east and south, and in the west towards Derby. The Green Belt also protects the separate identity of towns within the Erewash Valley and other main towns to the north of Nottingham, including Hucknall, Mansfield and Ashfield.

Stoke on Trent The Green Belt around Stoke-on-Trent and Newcastle-under-Lyme has limited the spread of the urban area; prevented coalescence with nearby towns like Congleton, Leek, Cheadle and Stone; and stimulated the regeneration of older industrial areas inside the Potteries conurbation. Much of this Green Belt is farmland and is attractive scenery, the north eastern sector being of particular landscape value, similar in character to the neighbouring Peak District National Park.

Gloucester and Cheltenham The purposes of this Green Belt are to protect the open character of the land between these two towns and to prevent them from merging. In 1981 the Gloucestershire Structure Plan extended the Green Belt north of Cheltenham to further protect the character of the town. The land in the Green Belt is almost all pleasant agricultural land at the foot of the Cotswold Hills, which are themselves designated as an Area of Outstanding Natural Beauty.

Fig. 21 The Oxford Green Belt from Boars Hill

Fig. 22 Beaulieu and the Beaulieu River in the South West Hampshire Green Belt

Bristol and Bath, also known as the Avon Green Belt and the Western Wiltshire Green Belt. All the main reasons for the establishment of a Green Belt apply in this case: to restrict the outward expansion of Bristol, to separate Bristol from Bath and to protect the special character of Bath. The landscape in the southern part of the Green Belt is very fine and the escarpment north of Bristol overlooking the river Severn is also attractive. The remainder is mainly pleasant farmland. Some extensions and minor boundary adjustments to the Green Belt were made when the Avon Structure Plan was approved in 1985, including the addition of attractive coastline between Clevedon and Portishead.

Oxford Oxford has become well known as a city with a dual personality. It is famous both as a university town and as a prosperous centre. The Green Belt seeks to prevent it from growing any bigger and to protect its character and setting. The landscape is not outstandingly attractive but it is intimate in scale and gentle in character. Most of it is average to good land used for mixed farming (Fig. 21).

Cambridge Cambridge also experiences the pressures of being both a university and a booming modern industrial town. There is a settled policy to limit its size, together with that of the surrounding villages. The Green Belt is one of the tools used to implement that policy and so help to preserve the city's character. The land is used for arable farming and is mainly flat but some higher ground to the west and the Gog Magog Hills to the south are also included.

South West Hampshire An area of Green Belt lies to the south west of the county. It is attractive country which includes the New Forest, the north shore of the Solent lying to the west of Southampton Water and the Beaulieu River (Fig. 22).

South East Dorset This Green Belt was established when the South East Dorset Structure Plan was approved in 1980. Its purposes are to contain the outward spread of the large built-up area of Poole, Bournemouth and Christchurch and to keep the separate identity of settlements. The Green Belt includes attractive river valleys, heathland and many wooded areas which are of recreational and nature conservation interest.

8   The Implications of a Green Belt

This Section has been revised, using the same headings, to take account of developments in other planning policies and procedures since 1962. The earlier passage on Decentralisation has been replaced by a new passage on Urban Regeneration.

The pressure on Green Belts There is a strong demand for more space for urban living. One of the many reasons is that despite pre-war forecasts of an eventual decline, the population of the country is still increasing. The number of separate households is growing even faster. There is plenty of work and greater prosperity, so that more people can afford separate and better homes. More land is required for new schools, hospitals and other public purposes, as well as for new roads and car parks to cope with the increasing traffic. If this need for more urban land encounters the restrictions implicit in a Green Belt, there are bound to be sharp increases in the value of building land and pressure to encroach on the Green Belts. Planning authorities and successive Ministers alike have resisted this pressure, have from time to time reiterated their intention to maintain the Green Belts and have supported their words by day to day decisions. They have done so while fully realising that land must be provided elsewhere to meet those needs which are not to be allowed in the Green Belt.

The allocation of building land The development plans prepared by local planning authorities (county councils and district councils) set out their policies for the development and other use of land in their areas. Pressure to build on land that is not allocated for development has mounted and land values have increased sharply wherever permission to build could be got. This has led to many requests for more land to be made available, often at the expense of a Green Belt.

Review of development plans Most county structure plans are now being reviewed. Such a review provides an opportunity to allocate more land for building if there is not enough already. In 1960 the Minister thought it advisable to issue a circular to local planning authorities on the subject. He said that he was anxious to see more land provided for development (where that did not conflict with important planning objectives) and to encourage fuller use of land within towns. Where a town was encircled by a Green Belt, adequate land should be selected beyond it, both for house building and for factories and offices. That policy guidance has been repeated on many occasions since 1960 and is just as relevant today.

The journey to work Fears have been expressed that the effect of a Green Belt will be to make people travel longer distances in their daily journey to work. This will, indeed, be so if the outward movement of people in search of homes is not accompanied by opportunities for employment. There are people who, though working in London or some other great city, choose to live at a distance and are prepared for the inconvenience and expense of a long daily journey. But most prefer work near their home if it can be got and the aim of policy is to bring about this freedom of choice.

Urban Regeneration The 1962 booklet pointed out that a Green Belt can be seen 'as a means of shaping the expansion of a city on a regional scale and not just an attempt to combat the forces making for growth'. The booklet emphasised the policy of decentralisation from London to New Towns and existing towns within and beyond the Green Belt. In the early plans of Unwin and Abercrombie (see pages 10 and 11 and Fig. 1) ample provision was made for new development at planned locations around the Green Belt.

Severe restrictions on building in the Green Belt still need to be matched with adequate provision for new development outside the Green Belt. That is the function of the land-use planning system, which is also the means of protecting the Green Belt itself. The Government, however, now places much more emphasis on the regeneration and redevelopment of the older urban areas than on decentralisation. This policy is implemented by encouraging the fullest use of land in urban areas, the reclamation of derelict land (Fig. 23), the release of unused land owned by local authorities and other public bodies, and by grants and other incentives to

Fig. 23 Housing on a reclaimed derelict coal mining site at Milking Bank Meadow, Dudley

developers willing to tackle derelict or difficult sites in the inner cities. For example, since 1979 the Government has:

* set up 10 Urban Development Corporations in England to undertake the regeneration of large derelict or run-down areas in London Docklands, Merseyside, Tyne & Wear, Teesside, the Black Country, Trafford, Central Manchester, Leeds and Sheffield. In total these cover over 40,000 acres.

* introduced new types of grant – now combined into City Grant – to stimulate major urban renewal schemes by private developers. Over the past 6 years nearly 300 grants totalling over £164m have been approved for schemes which will involve private sector investment of over £660m.

* set up 17 Enterprise Zones in England, most on largely derelict sites, where special grants and other incentives are available to encourage new development.

* established a Land Register of unused and underused land in public ownership with powers for the Secretary of State to direct the sale of sites for development. So far 159,000 acres have been entered on the Register and some 70,000 acres have been removed on being sold, brought into use or transferred to the private sector.

* greatly increased the resources available for the long established Derelict Land Grant system, which is resulting in the reclamation of around 2,400 acres a year, much of it in the inner cities.

In addition to these special schemes, the effective use of planning control over the use of undeveloped land has encouraged the 'recycling' of land in urban areas. Recent work by Ordnance Survey has shown that about 45% of land developed for housing in the past few years has been on sites that were formerly developed or on land within urban areas. More detailed surveys in the South East have shown that about 55% of new houses were on land of this kind.

The success of these policies is shown by the way in which the amount of agricultural land taken for development has declined dramatically in recent years and is now running at less than a third of the rate in the 1960s and 1970s, and only a quarter of the rate that it reached in the inter-war years and which led to the setting up of the first Green Belt around London.

9 The Maintenance and Improvement of a Green Belt

This Section is reproduced from the 1962 booklet.

The appearance of a Green Belt Once a Green Belt is defined the aim will usually be to maintain its rural appearance. Any buildings which are built there should be in keeping with the character of the area and this applies not only in the Green Belt itself but in any villages which lie within it, even though they may be formally excluded.

The powers of planning authorities to ensure that new building is in keeping with the rural appearance of the Green Belt are limited. They can say what shall not be done but they cannot say what shall be done, except as a condition of permission for some development or if they acquire the land themselves. Their principal weapon, the control of development, is essentially negative and however well it may be administered it is no substitute for good design in the first place. Planning authorities can control the external appearance of buildings and most of them take great care and trouble in doing so, but no statutory power can elicit a good design from a bad designer. Those who build have the responsibility of ensuring that what they build will be good to look at and nowhere is this more important than in Green Belt villages. But this does not mean that design of novel character is necessarily out of place. Authorities in deciding what to allow and what to reject have to distinguish between what is indifferent or illiterate and what is merely unusual. Designs which appear to conflict with what is there already often arouse indignation. This is quite understandable for few people welcome change, particularly in such an evocative setting as a village and a Green Belt village at that. But most villages and small towns contain buildings of all ages, which differ very much in character from one another but enrich each other by their contrasting styles and materials. So the modern building, if it is honestly designed, will in its turn enrich the village and should be welcomed. Attempts to maintain harmony by copying the styles of the past are seldom successful.

Minor structures, such as buildings incidental to the enjoyment of a dwelling house, and most agricultural buildings, are ordinarily exempt from planning control and Ministers are generally reluctant to withdraw these exemptions. Those who construct such buildings are relied upon to use care in their setting and design, so that they do not intrude on landscape or village. Nowhere is this more important than in a Green Belt. Nor is it only private developers who need to exercise care. Public authorities responsible for providing water, power, sewerage and roads carry their own responsibilities. They can do much by attention to detail and by the employment of skilled designers to lessen the impact of their works on the countryside. The rural appearance of a Green Belt is easily destroyed by man-made objects used for public works, some of which might be appropriate enough in a nearby suburb. Concrete kerbs, lamp posts and fences, tangles of overhead wires, standard traffic bollards and the treatment of an open space as though it were a town park are some examples.

Fig. 24 The River Thames at Laleham

Public authorities of one kind or another can do a lot to maintain and improve the appearance of a Green Belt and its usefulness for recreation. They can acquire land for public enjoyment, construct car parks, plant trees and open up views over the countryside from some favoured vantage point. They can remove disused buildings and reclaim derelict land. They can fill worked-out mineral pits with refuse and restore the land to use. They can improve and maintain footpaths and bridle ways and provide sign-posts for those that have been determined as public rights of way.

The role of the individual The appearance of the Green Belt depends also on the activities of numberless individuals. The planning authority can prevent buildings being erected but they cannot ensure that land is used for agriculture; they can stop trees being felled or fine buildings from being demolished, but they cannot ensure the proper maintenance of woodlands or the repair of a building which is not a public danger. The residents and landowners in the Green Belt can contribute substantially to its maintenance or destruction, but its appearance depends to an even greater extent on the relations between those who live and work there and those who use it for their recreation, for riding, cycling, walking, motoring, fishing, sailing, boating, shooting or hunting (Fig. 24). Many of these activities imply some conflict with agriculture. The very presence of large numbers of town dwellers, even if they scrupulously follow the Country Code*, means some

---

* See *Out in the Country*, Countryside Commission, 1987.

disturbance. If there is trespass or pilfering, the farmer will be antagonized. Furthermore, the townsman requires some concessions from the farmer for his satisfaction in the beauty of the landscape, such as care in the siting and design of farm buildings and the preservation of trees. So the maintenance of the Green Belt is not only a matter of control by the planning authority but also a question of how it is used by people in search of recreation and of how the land is managed by public and private landowners.

The public are entitled to expect that, once a Green Belt is established, the authorities concerned will effectively carry out any policies necessary to its maintenance as a belt of open country and to the enhancement of its rural appearance. But public authorities in a democratic country cannot for long pursue a policy which does not have public support. So the future of a Green Belt depends in the end on public opinion. This requires understanding of the issues involved. The function of a Green Belt as a place for the recreation and enjoyment of all is well understood. It differs from, though it does not conflict with, its function as a means of shaping the expansion of a town or group of towns. The former may have more appeal but the latter is the primary purpose of a Green Belt. The aim of this booklet has been to explain why this is so and thus to contribute to that informed public opinion on which the future depends.

Further reading
Green Belts by Martin J. Elson (Heinemann, London, 1986) provides a comprehensive account of Green Belt history and policy, and includes full references to journal articles and other relevant publications.

Annex Control over Development in Green Belts

The following is an extract from Planning Policy Guidance Note No. 2 on Green Belts (paras 12–18).

12. The general policies controlling development in the countryside apply with equal force in Green Belts but there is, in addition, a general presumption against inappropriate development within them.

13. Inside a Green Belt, approval should not be given, except in very special circumstances, for the construction of new buildings or for the change of use of existing buildings for purposes other than agriculture and forestry, outdoor sport, cemeteries, institutions standing in extensive grounds, or other uses appropriate to a rural area.

14. Structure and local planning policies should make no reference to the possibility of allowing other development in exceptional circumstances. Nor should the visual amenities of the Green Belt be injured by proposals for development within or conspicuous from the Green Belt which, although they would not prejudice its main purpose, might be inappropriate by reason of their siting, materials or design.

15. Minerals can be worked only where they are found. Their extraction need not be incompatible with Green Belt objectives, provided that high environmental standards are maintained and that the site is well restored.

16. Green Belts contain a large number of substantial and attractive agricultural buildings which, with normal repair and maintenance, can be expected to last for many years. When these are no longer needed for farming, the planning authority will need to consider whether they might be appropriately re-used for other purposes which help to diversify the rural economy. Redundant agricultural buildings can provide suitable accommodation for small firms or tourist activities or can be used as individual residences. The re-use of redundant buildings should not be refused unless there are specific and convincing reasons which cannot be overcome by attaching conditions to the planning permission.

17. In the next few years many older hospitals located in Green Belts are likely to become redundant. In planning for the future of these buildings and their sites the aim should be to use them for purposes compatible with the Green Belt, which can include institutional uses. The size, layout and form of the buildings may, however, make them unsuitable for such purposes. In such cases it will be necessary to consider whether very special circumstances exist that would warrant the change of use of the buildings or the construction of new buildings.

18. In some cases it may be possible to convert the existing buildings for housing or other uses, perhaps with some demolition of ancillary buildings. But if that is not a practical solution then the future of the buildings and the site, and the possibility of redevelopment, will need to be carefully considered. Putting the sites to beneficial use will be preferable to allowing the buildings to remain empty and the site to become derelict.

The Note also gives detailed guidelines for future use of redundant hospital sites in Green Belts.